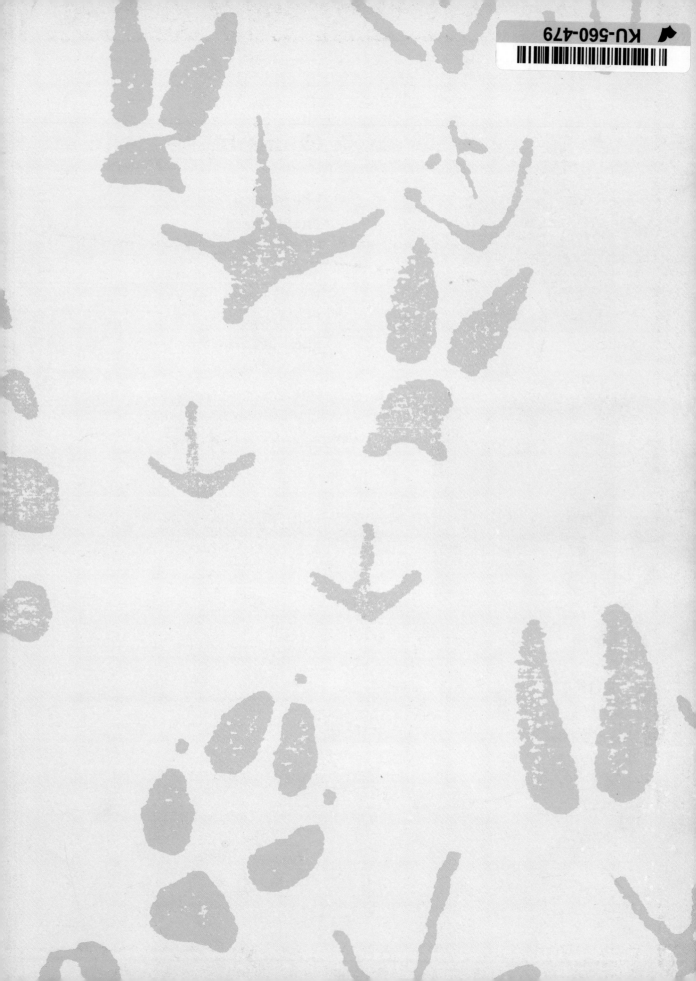

Contents

A MACDONALD BOOK

© Hachette, Paris, 1986

First published in France in 1986 by
Hachette Jeunesse
as *Animaux des Bois et des Forêts*

First published in Great Britain in 1987 by
Macdonald & Company (Publishers) Ltd
London & Sydney
A BPCC plc company

All rights reserved

Printed and bound in France

Macdonald & Company (Publishers) Ltd
Greater London House
Hampstead Road
London NW1 7QX

Credits
This edition produced for Macdonald Publishers by
Lionheart Books,
10 Chelmsford Square, London NW10 3AR.

Translated by Madeleine Bender
Adapted by Lionel Bender
Artwork services by Radius

British Library Cataloguing in Publication Data
Bender, Lionel
   Woods and forests.—(Nature notes; 3)
   1. Forest fauna—Europe—Juvenile
literature
   I. Title II. Bender, Madeleine III. Series
   591.94   QL253

ISBN 0-356-11994-7

Nature Notes

WOODS AND FORESTS

Translated by Madeleine Bender
Adapted by Lionel Bender

Many different animals are found in woods. To get close to them you have to be very careful and quiet. Learn to walk noiselessly and avoid treading on dead twigs and branches, which will snap easily with a loud crack. Position yourself downwind of the animals. Speak to the forest wardens to find the best places to hide and the best times to observe each species. Learn how to recognize tracks as these are the first clues to locating elusive animals.

Whenever you set out to discover wildlife in woods and forests, be sure to wear the right clothes and to take the right equipment: dull-coloured wind- or waterproof clothing, sturdy shoes, a pair of binoculars, a knife, a pencil and a notebook in which to write or draw. You may also wish to take a camera and a guide book to identify plants, trees and birds.

The animals will then become familiar through what you have seen, heard, drawn and recorded, and you will appreciate the richness of wildlife in these habitats, often not too far from our cities and towns.

The Marten

A DISCREET PRESENCE

If there is an animal that is difficult to observe, it is indeed the marten. Always discreet, it never goes near built-up areas. Furthermore, it hunts mostly at night and searches for food within a vast territory. By day it rests in tree hollows or abandoned nests.

However, the marten can be found in all the large forest areas of Europe. It prefers to make its home in a vast and deep forest with very tall trees.

The marten has a lithe body and alert eyes. It is the size of a cat and has a brown coat and a long bushy tail. A light patch below the throat, the bib, is creamy white tinged with orange. The underparts are greyish. The short legs end with strong claws that are used for climbing. The female is slightly larger than the male.

AN EXCELLENT TREE CLIMBER

Adapted, above all, to life in trees, the marten climbs better than the cat. It jumps from one tree to another in leaps of more than four metres and can come down tree trunks head-first. It is the only mammal capable of catching up with a squirrel in tree branches. In many regions the squirrel is in fact its main prey. But the marten also feeds on other woodland rodents, birds, eggs and, occasionally, insects and berries.

NEW GENERATIONS

In April the female generally gives birth to three young that it suckles for six to eight weeks. At the age of about three months the young martens start following their mother on her hunting trips and stay with her until autumn.

The light tracks of the marten are not often seen.

They are mature when only a year old and produce their first litters when two years old. Martens can live to about seventeen years.

DIFFICULT TO FOLLOW

The marten is one of the animals whose habits are least known. It is very shy. Its vision, hearing and sense of smell are exceptionally keen and allow it to detect a strange presence from a great distance.

The marten's tracks are not easy to follow. Being lightweight, this animal does not leave deep footprints. Also, since most of its life is spent in trees it leaves very few tracks.

The marten's hearing is so well developed that it can pick up the sounds made by a mouse. Its sense of smell is as acute as a dog's. And it can see even in the darkest night. It is at dusk and late at night that its hunting trips are the most successful.

THE SQUIRREL'S ENEMY

Should a gust of wind bring to the marten's nostrils the scent of a squirrel sleeping in its drey, the marten climbs to the top of the tree, makes a hole in the drey and devours the squirrel in a few mouthfuls

If the night is very dark, the squirrel does not stand a chance of escaping. If, however, there is enough light for the squirrel to see its way about, a mad pursuit takes place. The marten is as good a climber as the squirrel and it can also leap from branch to branch, using its tail both for balance and direction. But the squirrel has its escape tactics. It climbs higher and higher, up where the thin branches cannot support the greater weight of the marten.

THE FRAGILE BALANCE OF THE FOREST

Squirrels often fall victim to the marten's appetite, but, surprisingly, it is

Fascinated by an object left in full view, the marten is then easy to observe... if you move away a little.

when there are no martens left that the squirrel population drops, hit by a mysterious disease. The marten attacks sick or weak squirrels first. By getting rid of these animals the marten helps to stop epidemics.

Sportsmen complain that the marten consumes large numbers of game birds. Indeed it does, but in a lot of hunting grounds pheasants and partridges are bred like farmyard chickens just so the guests are assured of bringing back some game. When the birds are released on the day before the 'shoot' begins, they do not know how to protect themselves in their new environment. The marten and the other predators have a memorable feast.

In autumn the marten feeds on berries and fruit. In winter it becomes carnivorous again and preys on birds and on rodents that do not hibernate.

VICTIM TO ITS BEAUTY

In the old days, smart women used to wear fur stoles. The marten's fur, which is particularly beautiful and thick, was very much sought after. The marten was hunted or trapped in winter to the extent that it disappeared from many forests. Its plight was made worse by the fact that it is easily caught.

Today it has become necessary to protect this animal as well as all the other members of the Mustelidae family, the otter, ermine, badger and skunk. These small mammals, all of which are threatened by our activities, play a part in the balance of nature.

The marten's diet is varied. It prefers meat but eats fruit and berries as well.

The Buzzard

A FAMILIAR BIRD OF PREY

The buzzard often perches close to the ground, keeping a look-out for rodents. At other times, very high in the sky, it glides and flies slowly in wide circles, letting out a shrill, plaintive cry similar to the miaowing of a cat: in German, the buzzard is called the eagle-cat. You can then observe the bird's stout body, its wide wings slightly turned up at the tip, the primary wing feathers separated like fingers and its rounded tail that bears about a dozen dark bands of colour.

The buzzard's plumage varies in colour from one individual to another but is generally dark brown on the back and brown with white spots underneath. Some buzzards, though, are completely mid-brown, other are beige with almost white underparts.

AN UNTIDY NEST

Like the nest of another bird of prey, the eagle, the buzzard's nest is called an eyrie. It is most often a loose structure of twigs and branches lined with leaves, moss and wool, built at the top of a tall tree on the edge of the forest. The location of the eyrie is usually given away by the bird's courtship display carried out high in the sky above. The pair glide in circles around each other then soar, tumble and loop the loop, all the time strengthening the bond between them.

In April, the female lays two, three or four eggs that are white with brown spots. She incubates the eggs for about a month. At first only the male goes off to find food for the young while the female stands guard but later they take it in turns, bringing back mainly small

rodents and chicks of other species.

As well as voles and field mice, the buzzard feeds on moles, snakes, lizards, frogs, insects, molluscs and occasionally small game or dead animals.

The buzzard feeds mainly on field and meadow rodents

BE CAREFUL ALONG THE MOTORWAY

Along the motorways that pass through certain major European forests there are road signs indicating the presence of birds of prey. The species that they refer to is most probably the buzzard. Dozens of buzzards are killed each year by passing vehicles and a bird of this size represents a real danger for the motorist driving at high speeds.

With a bit of luck, you will see a buzzard perched on a fence-post or a bush. Sitting motionless, with its head tucked in between its shoulders and its feathers puffed up, it looks asleep. Through binoculars, you may see the great dark bird suddenly dive on its prey, flying down with half-closed wings, kill the animal with a quick stroke of its beak and carry it away in its

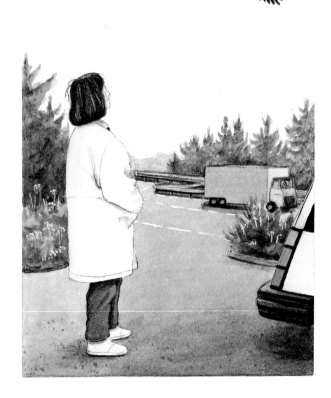

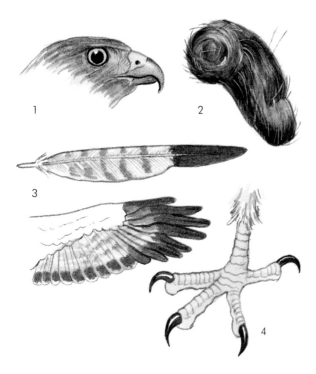

Hooked beak (1)   regurgitation pellets (2)   long primary feathers (3)   sharp talons (4)   are special features of birds of prey.

talons to devour it.

After its meal, the buzzard regurgitates pellets consisting of the parts of its prey it cannot digest, such as bones, hair and fur.

PUTTING A STOP TO THE SLAUGHTER

Some fifty years ago in Britain the buzzard population was on the increase. Then in 1954 rabbits, an important part of its diet, were stricken by the disease myxomatosis. The buzzard and many other animals that preyed largely on rabbits, went hungry. The population never recovered although now numbers are steady.

Today, despite being protected by law, buzzards can still be found caught in traps, fighting for their lives.

Out of all the birds of prey, the buzzard is the one hunters and country folk are most inclined to kill. They accuse it of eating game and plundering chicken coops; in parts of France the buzzard is called the hen-chaser.

Finally, in some countries buzzards fall victim to shop keepers who do not respect the law of wildlife conservation; in shopwindows and restaurants stuffed buzzards can be seen holding a rabbit or a partridge in their talons, reinforcing the idea that the buzzard is a pest.

A MISUNDERSTOOD BIRD

In reality, the buzzard eats very few game animals. It is mostly the sick or old members of a population that it catches, and usually only in winter, when its normal prey are scarce.

Even though it can be a nuisance in stealing chickens, the buzzard also has a beneficial role in nature. Each year it helps to preserve tonnes of grain that would otherwise be eaten by voles. One vole, at harvest time, accumulates an average of one kilo of grain in its burrow and one pair of buzzards destroys about 6 000 voles a year. You can calculate the saving for yourself.

Events that took place in 1983, near Pontarlier, in the Jura region of France, proved beyond all shadow of a doubt the usefulness of buzzards. Following the buzzard's almost complete destruction by hunters, farmers saw their meadows and fields devastated by voles' and fieldmice's burrows and tunnels. After attempting, without success, to stem the invasion of these small rodents, pairs of buzzards were reintroduced and the law forbidding their killing enforced. Since then, voles and fieldmice have been far less numerous in the area and farmers' crop outputs have soared.

The Wild Boar

A POWERFUL ANIMAL

With a fat, thick-set body and a large head with a mobile snout, the wild boar is an ancestor of the domestic pig. It lives in large forests. Its eyes are small and bright, and its earflaps, covered with rough bristles, can swivel round. Its stout neck bears a mane that stands on end when the animal is surprised or angry. Its highly mobile tail ends in a little tuft of hair.

Its colour changes from dark brown to light grey according to the seasons. In autumn, a thick underfur grows that is covered with long, dark, tough hairs, the bristles. In spring, the underfur is shed and the bristles grow again but now shorter and lighter in colour.

Before winter, under its skin, the boar accumulates a layer of fat that it uses as a food reserve but also acts as protection against the cold. The adult male's skin is very thick on the shoulders; this sort of armour protects it from the bites of its enemies and the tusks of rival wild boars when they fight.

A CARING MOTHER

At the end of winter the pregnant female goes off on her own and, in a nest of grasses, dead leaves and branches, gives birth to between two and six young. The piglets are born with their eyes open and have a series of light and dark stripes on their back such that their coat provides excellent camouflage. They start following their mother straight away. The mother, or sow, goes on suckling them until they are about three months old. She confronts any enemy or aggressor if she feels her young are in danger.

GETTING TO KNOW THE WILD BOAR BETTER

Mostly nocturnal in its habits, the wild boar is difficult to observe. It is also rather wary of people. By day, it cannot be seen, retreating into the depth of a thicket where it lies in its lair or wallows in a muddy puddle or pond. When surprised, it chooses to run away rather than stand its ground. It is a remarkable long-distance runner. On its short legs, which bear strong hooves, it can reach a speed of forty kilometres an hour and can keep this up for many minutes.

Should you visit a forest where wild boars live, you are likely to come in close contact with them without realizing it. A frightened blackbird makes more noise than a boar as it flees! If by some stroke of luck you catch a glimpse of a wild boar, perhaps at the end of a long, narrow path, do not run away. It is a peaceful animal that does not like to be disturbed and it will not blindly charge anything that moves.

THE BOAR'S HEAD

The wild boar's strength as well as its cleverness is concentrated in its head. Its snout and tusks together form a superb digging tool that it uses in its search for food. In males the tusks are particularly large and are used as weapons.

Guided by its very keen sense of smell, the boar digs the earth with its snout, looking for acorns and earthworms. Along woodland footpaths you can often find patches of dug up earth and grass that show its ploughing activities. On the banks of ponds and marshes it thrusts its snout underground to pull up the roots of

An old male in its winter coat

A young piglet is easy to tame

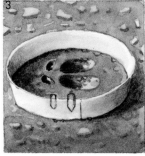

The stages in the making of a track cast:
1 – clean the track of debris
2 – brush with oil to make it easier to remove the plaster
3 – surround the track with a cylinder of cardboard pushed into the earth   4 – pour in the moulding plaster
5 – allow to dry for one hour, take out the plaster cast, and clean everything.

reeds, leaving behind funnel-shaped holes in the mud. It crushes the roots in its powerful jaws.

Unfortunately, its healthy appetite often takes it, in the night, into cultivated fields. Young cereals, corn, and potatoes are all to its liking, and the wild boar sometimes causes a lot of damage to valuable crops. In many areas it is considered a pest, especially as it breeds well and has few natural enemies to keep its numbers down.

CUNNING, COURAGE, INTELLIGENCE

Because of its liking for crops, the wild boar is hunted without mercy. However, this remarkably intelligent animal knows how to defend itself particularly well. Its instinct points it in the direction of safe places and paths in the forest and it often escapes the traps set by hunters. If it feels cornered by the dogs the hunters use to track it down, it confronts them head-on.

Gamekeepers often find newborn wild boar piglets next to their dead mother. If the gamekeepers bottle-feed the piglets, they soon become tame, answer to their name, come to be stroked and frolic like puppies. Alas, these piglets soon grow too large and cumbersome to keep as pets.

MARKS OF ITS PASSAGE

Dug up and ploughed soil and tree bark worn smooth by its constant rubbing to get rid of parasites on its skin are marks of the wild boar's activities. By examining the tracks it leaves in the ground, forest wardens can describe the animal without having seen it: its sex, its weight, its age, its appearance. How amazing!

Bark Beetles

STRANGE PATTERNS

In the hedgerow a tree is dead. Part of the bark has fallen and on the trunk a strange pattern marks the activities of an insect. Many elm and ash trees bear this mark.

In a forest, an oak, a pine, a fir and a birch have all been attacked in this way. From the outside, small heaps of sawdust around cracks in the bark or at the foot of the tree indicate the presence of the destroyers. On taking a closer look you can see that the patterns created by these harmful sculptors are different. They are the distinctive mark of an insect that knows how to recognize different species of tree and to live at the tree's expense. On the trunk a round chamber with galleries radiating from it indicates the presence of a species that has laid eggs in the wood. The larvae have burrowed outwards from the centre of the chamber. In other examples, a central tunnel gives access to galleries radiating out at right angles. All this takes place between bark and wood. It is the work of the bark beetles.

A VERY SMALL INSECT

The adult insect measures between two and seven millimetres in length. It is black or brown and cylinder-shaped. It feeds on the tree's sap. The female lays its eggs in the wood. Each egg hatches a white larva, or grub, which feeds on the wood. The larva changes into a nymph, then an adult insect that will bore through the bark at the end of its gallery to escape from the tree. All the adult insects come out at the same time, creating a swarm capable of breeding very quickly.

DANGEROUS ENGRAVINGS

In the forest, the bark of a fallen pine tree comes off in large pieces. Patterns can be seen here and there on the inner surfaces of the bark. Matching patterns also appear on the surface of the wood. A closer look reveals they are the two halves of a network. On the wood each groove is filled with sawdust and it is this that creates a raised pattern.

If you lift up such a piece of bark to the sun, you can see a ray of light coming through a small hole. It is the entrance to the primary or main tunnel. In the secondary or side tunnels the entrance is narrower than the far end. If the tree has not been down too long, you may discover a white grub at the end of a tunnel. This is the beetle larva hatched from an egg deposited at the entrance of the tunnel by the female bark beetle. The female pierced the bark, dug the central tunnel and laid eggs along it on both sides. It laid as many eggs as there are side tunnels. As the larvae bore out the side tunnels they grow and as they do so they gradually enlarge their lodgings. That is why the side galleries are wider at the end.

To find out how many insects laid their eggs along the tree trunk you have to count the patterns. You only have to look at the appearance of trees around to spot the ones that have been attacked. The needles are turning yellow, the branches are dying, the tree is wasting away rapidly.

Place a sheet of paper over the wood and with a pencil, a piece of charcoal or even some damp earth, trace the pattern by gently rubbing against the paper. This magnificent engraving, however, means that the forest as a whole is in poor condition as the bark beetles only

The light comes through the entrance hole of the main gallery.

Trace the bark beetle's pattern.

attack trees already weakened by, for example, lack of water, deep cuts or pollution. A beetle's attack is the death warrant of the tree as it eats the tree's very essence.

A CLANDESTINE CARRIER OF DISEASE

Bark beetles are often talked about as these small insects recently managed to destroy almost all the elms of Europe. When getting into the tree, the elm bark beetle carries the spores of a microscopic fungus that causes a fatal disease in the tree: Dutch elm disease. At the same time as the bark beetles bore into the wood, the fungus invades the tree's sap carrying vessels and blocks them, causing the death of the tree within only a few weeks.

A terrible cycle of events leads the forest to its doom. Industry produces acid gases that weaken the trees, and this weakness favours the settlement of bark beetles that carry the deadly fungus from tree to tree.

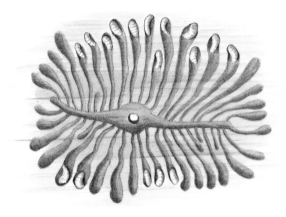

SUBLETTING

At the end of a gallery there is a dried up larva. If you look at it through a magnifying glass its body seems to have burst open. Ichneumon flies, which look like slim wasps, or ant-beetles, which are very similar in appearance to ants, have deposited their eggs in the body of the bark beetle's larva. It has been used as shelter and food for the larvae of these parasites!

Woodpeckers, nuthatches, and tree-creepers also play a part in the destruction of bark beetles in their adult or larval states.

Pollution weakens the forest, the bark beetles move in, the trees waste away.

The Common Jay

A PRETTY COUSIN OF THE CROWS

The jay is classified as a member of the crow family. It differs from other crows in size – at about thirty centimetres in length it is the smallest in the family – and colour – its plumage is pinkish brown.

In flight it spreads its broad rounded wings, which have white markings and a patch of blue feathers barred with black. Its tail is almost black, its rump white, and its crown bears black, white and brown feathers. It is easy to see these colours as the jay's flight is slow. Male and female look alike; only their behaviour tells them apart.

The jay builds its nest mostly in oak woods. Its beak, which is slightly hooked, is strong enough to break twigs. It arranges the twigs in the fork of main branches or at the top of a young tree. It lines the nest with roots and dried grass, and although the nest is very roughly made, it is well hidden.

In May, the female lays four to six eggs, which are greenish-brown with brown spots. The eggs hatch about two weeks later. The young are fed by both parents. They leave the nest three weeks later but stay with the family group until autumn.

A VARIED DIET

While it is feeding its young, the jay catches a huge number of wasps, crickets, caterpillars, spiders and large beetles. It is estimated that, while they are in the nest, the young birds each devour several thousand insects. The jay sometimes even brings to its brood some eggs or small birds taken from another species' nest.

In spite of its reputation for plundering nests, the jay gets most of its food from around the oak tree close to which it always stays.

SPREADING TREES

In autumn, it gathers acorns. Some of these it eats straight away, the rest it buries under moss or divides up and hides in various caches. To make a cache, it pecks a hole in the ground with its beak, places an acorn in it and then covers the hole with earth. In winter it occasionally visits these food stores but seems to forget the location of some of them. Unknowingly, therefore, the jay plays a part in the spreading of oaks.

In winter, the jay also feeds on beech masts, hazelnuts, fruit and wild berries.

The jay spreads acorns around the forest.

When danger is near the jay sounds the alarm.

A SENTRY

In forests, the jay rarely leaves the tree cover and its presence there cannot go unnoticed as it is very noisy. A raucous, grating cry silences the blackbirds and the tits. The jay has warned them of the approach of an intruder – yourself or perhaps a hunting bird of prey.

Perched on a branch, its neck outstretched, its crest raised, the jay's excitement often also signals the unfolding of a tragedy: the rabbit caught by a fox or the marten plundering a bird's nest.

Hunters are not fond of this bird since it gives away their silent approach.

A MIMIC

Often seen gathered in small groups, jays chatter, cheep and cluck, vocally trying to outdo each other. They are

Years ago, the jay used to be a pet of country folk. Today it is still possible to tame it.

To build its nest the jay looks for twigs, dry grass and small roots.

past masters in the art of mimicking other birds; a jay has been known to hoot like an owl every time it flew past a tree where a tawny owl roosted.

In the past, in the country, a young jay that had fallen from the nest would be captured and reared on a farm. During its captivity, the young bird would soon become a pet and clown around in the house. Curious by nature, it would observe, perched on the top of a cupboard, the comings and goings in the kitchen, its light-blue eyes sparkling. It would mimic to perfection the cat's miaowing, while always staying well away from the animal. In the farmyard it would share the dog's meal and was able to earn its respect with a peck of its powerful beak.

Some jays, probably more gifted than others, could even talk. From the back of their throat, with their beak closed, they would manage to utter a few words, always the same ones, at the most unlikely times.

AN OLD LEGEND

In oak woods you can often find one of the small blue and black feathers lost by the jay during moulting or fighting. Treat it with care. On returning home, look at it through a magnifying glass. The fine barbs are of an extraordinary blue, a blue unique in nature.

Would you like to know how the jays found such a pure blue? An old legend says that a long time ago all the snakes would meet one night in spring each year to make a fabulous blue diamond with their saliva. One day, the jay learnt about this, stole the snakes' diamond and took it to its nest. Since that day, the legend says, the bird uses it to colour its wings!

The Adder

SEE AND RECOGNIZE…

The adder, or northern viper, is the most common of British snakes, but is absent from Ireland and some Scottish islands. Usually seen in dry places such as sandy heaths, sunny slopes of hills, logs, piles of stones, it prefers to keep away from noise and bustle.

In size, it measures from about 40 to 75 centimetres in length. Females tend to be slightly longer than males.

Its colour varies from yellowy brown to rusty brown and it has marble-like darker geometric markings along the whole length of its body. The dark zig-zag line along its back ends at its neck, and its head has the familiar v-shape mark. The rather short tail is distinct from the rest of the body by its almost total lack of markings.

The adder is rather unique among snakes in that the male and female are coloured differently. Males are usually cream, yellow or olive-grey with black markings and a black or speckled white throat. Females tend to be red, reddish-brown or gold with dark red or brown markings and a yellowish-white chin.

The adder crawls rather slowly with long, horizontal wave-like movements of its body. The broad scales on its underside are so arranged that the snake cannot move backwards: this one-way motion design is now used in the making of the soles of cross-country skis.

…RELATIVE DANGER

The adder does not attack people. It is a rather shy animal and flees at the slightest noise. However, if you step on it, it will defend itself and can then be dangerous as it possesses two venomous

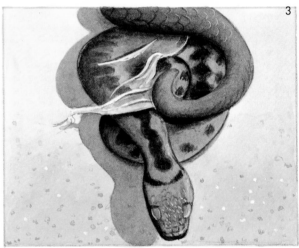

The adder is ovoviviparous: the eggs (1) hatch inside the mother (2) and the young come out live in a membrane (3).

fangs that are always ready to strike with lightning speed.

The danger the adder presents compared to that of, say, a cobra, does not justify its massacre. It is in fact a useful animal in nature, eating rats, voles and other rodents that destroy crops, and as such is protected. In the British Isles, in the last eighty years or so there have been only seven recorded deaths due to snake bites. If you happen to get bitten by an adder, do not panic: avoid running or moving about and get someone to take you to the nearest doctor.

When walking in a place where adders live, wear heavy shoes or boots and keep your eyes peeled. You might be lucky and see an adder, curled up on a flat stone in the sun on the look-out for a rat or a field mouse.

LEGENDS AND REALITY

Out of all the animals in the world, snakes are probably the ones with the worst reputation. When you talk about adders, there are few people who do not have a shiver of fear or distaste.

The adder is said to fascinate birds so much that it can hypnotise them. This is not true. However, birds may be temporarily transfixed by the snake's eyes, which move very little and are covered by a fixed membrane.

Spiteful scandal-mongers are said to have a "viperish tongue". The snake's tongue, however, is completely harmless. Indeed it is forked and looks rather menacing but it is not a sting as some people imagine. It plays no part in the injecting of venom and is merely a smell and taste organ.

The adder is also said to climb trees, to rear up on its tail, to hiss when it is

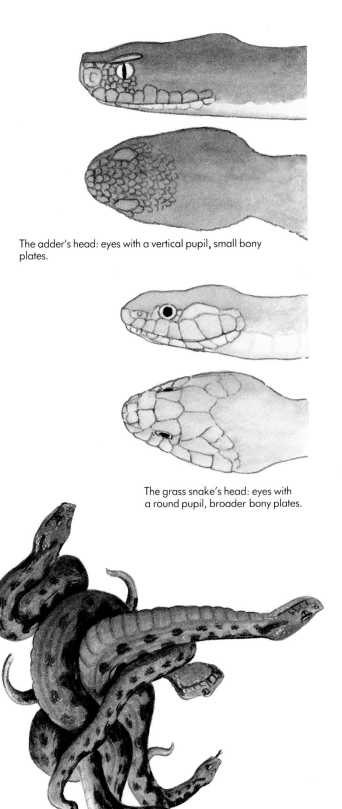

The adder's head: eyes with a vertical pupil, small bony plates.

The grass snake's head: eyes with a round pupil, broader bony plates.

angry and so on. It is quite common, in the country, to hear people say that adders come in the night to milk cows. This, though, is impossible as the adder's jaws do not allow it to suck.

Legends like this are easy to disprove. Haven't you also heard that adders are able to rush after people and catch up with them as they run away across fields and jump over ditches? Isn't it reassuring to know that this reptile can only crawl horizontally and that its maximum speed cannot exceed eight kilometres an hour.

THE DANCE OF THE ADDERS

In the warmer parts of Europe, where adders are more numerous, in the first sunny weeks of April a curious phenomenon takes place. In answer to a mysterious signal, probably a subtle smell, all the adders within a distance of several hundred metres converge on the same point – perhaps around a pile of stones or on a sunny mound in a meadow. Here they intertwine to form a wriggling mass twenty or so centimetres in diameter. The snakes knot and unknot repeatedly for several hours. This is the nuptual parade of the adders.

In Britain, at the beginning of the breeding season males can often be seen swaying together, their bodies entwined. Each tries to force the other to the ground, but they do not bite one another. This climax of the territorial rivalry between males is referred to as the dance of the adders. At the end of the dance, one male gives up and goes away. The victor will mate with the female, which has usually been waiting close by. About two months later the female gives birth to between five and twenty young.

The European Roe Deer

ELEGANT AND SPIRITED

Even if the roe deer is among the smallest of the deer living in Europe, it certainly is the most graceful of our forest dwellers. It particularly likes woods with fairly thick undergrowth.

Very fast on its legs, it can run at a speed of more than eighty kilometres an hour and cover a distance of four metres with each bound. Its legs are long and slim, its body dainty and slender, its neck long and slim, and its head is large and bears dark eyes and large cone-shaped ears.

The colour of its coat varies with the seasons: reddish-brown in summer and greyish-brown in winter. Under its very short tail there is a white patch that is particularly obvious in winter and the hairs of which are raised to form a 'powder-puff' when the deer is alarmed.

The head of the male roe deer, the buck, bears antlers, which are the 'horns' of deer. Every year, in late autumn, the antlers are shed and new ones that are stronger and more beautiful grow in their place. The female, the doe, has no antlers.

The doe generally gives birth to two young, the kids. The kids' spotted coat makes them difficult to see in the dappled light of the undergrowth. They have to escape the many natural dangers within the forest if they are to become adults. Their spots will disappear after one year.

The buck marks its territory by cutting, with its antlers, deep vertical grooves in the trunk of certain trees. It also rubs its antlers against trees to try to get rid of its 'velvet', the very thin skin that covers its antlers while they are growing. Near a tree you may find

The roe deer's leaps can be several metres long.

pieces of velvet but you will be extremely fortunate to find the antlers themselves; these the deer sheds every autumn.

If by chance you encounter a kid, don't try to touch it! It has not been abandoned. Its mother is watching over it, close by. The kid is not in any great danger as it has no scent and its spotted coat is a perfect camouflage. Once marked with your scent, on the other hand, it would become prey for the fox, the wild cat or the stray dog.

IF YOU SEE IT

Right in the middle of a path a roe deer, surprised by your appearance in its territory, freezes and looks at you. Do not move. If you do, the deer will leap into the tall grass, with its legs outstretched, back arched and head held high, in a great noise of broken branches. As it leaps it may utter a barking noise, which is surprisingly similar to a dog's bark.

GETTING CLOSE TO THE ROE DEER

To get close to it you need to know its way of life. Provided there is enough food in its territory, the roe deer never ventures beyond its boundaries. It grazes on open grassland, picking up items of food here and there. It does not cause much damage to crops. On the other hand, it is very fond of young trees, biting off the new shoots with its teeth, which damages new plantations.

The best times to observe the roe deer are in the evening, when it comes into the open to graze, and at dawn, when it wanders about in the undergrowth looking for a place to rest. However, it is possible to encounter the roe deer during the day; because it has a small stomach it needs to eat every few hours.

The roe deer is a very cautious animal. It can smell you from a distance of more than 100 metres. You must therefore approach it by keeping downwind of it at all times as the wind carries scents and sounds. The roe deer

1 – A buck in 'velvet'.
2 – Roe deer antlers reach a maximum length of 15 to 20 cm.
3 – A hoof print.
4 – A tree scraped by a roe deer.

has a very keen sense of hearing: the snapping of a twig under your feet is enough to make it run away. Its vision, on the other hand, is only average, and you will be able to watch it if you remain motionless.

The best vantage points are the edges of clearings, the boundaries of woods or where several paths cross. Wear neutral-coloured clothes, never come out of woods abruptly, hunch yourself up, and scan clearings carefully before entering them.

NUMEROUS SIGNS LEFT BEHIND

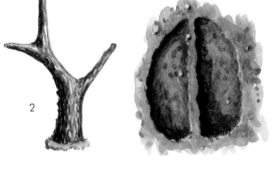

Before lying in wait for long periods, you must make sure there is a roe deer around. Fortunately, the animal often follows the same paths, occupies a territory that is not very large, and leaves behind several signs. These signs include the tracks left by its hooves in the damp earth and droppings either scattered among the tracks or in large heaps. You may also see a 'roe ring', the ring or figure of eight worn in the ground around a tree as the buck chases the doe before mating.

The Nuthatch

AN ACROBATIC CLIMBER

The nuthatch is a climbing bird that lives mainly in the old trees of deciduous woods. It can also be found in town parks and often even in gardens with many trees. The nuthatch builds its nest in holes in trees.

The size of a sparrow, it has a compact body and a stumpy tail that gives it a distinctive look especially when at rest; the head then forms a straight line with the back. The top of its body and wings are blue-grey, its underparts are orangy yellow and its flanks buff with a reddish tinge. The female is paler on the flanks than the male and the young are duller.

The nuthatch is the only bird that can go down a tree-trunk head-first. It does not need to use its tail as a support; its strong feet, bearing powerful claws, are enough for it to hold on and keep its balance in almost any position. You can therefore see it travelling downwards, upwards, sideways on the trunk and even under big branches.

It flies with quick, flitting actions over short distances.

A SEDENTARY BIRD

The nuthatch stays in the same area all year round provided there is enough food. In winter nuthatch pairs often join flocks of tits to feed. But it is in spring that we notice it most, hearing its call: "chwit, chwit, chwit".

Numerous, quite bold and rather inquisitive, nuthatches are easy to see at that time of the year. As early as April, the male and female look for a woodpecker's old nest in a tree, a hole between two stones of a building or a nesting box. The pair line the chosen nest with dead leaves and bark.

The female nuthatch, the hen, lays her eggs at the rate of one per day for about a week. She incubates the eggs straight away. The male feeds the hen at the nest. During the whole of the two-week incubation period the birds remain silent so as not to attract predators or inquisitive people.

Most pairs produce just a single brood during the breeding season.

WHO'S KNOCKING ON THE TREE?

On an April morning a loud "toc-toc-toc" rings out in the forest. It comes from the tree just a little way ahead. So clear and strong is the pecking sound that you expect to find quite a large bird at the tree. But it is only the nuthatch, picking insects from under the bark.

The nuthatch feeds on insects, hazelnuts and beechnuts. It fixes the nuts in a crevice in the tree bark and hammers them open with its beak to get to the kernel, swinging its body with each blow. The remains of its meals can be found in various 'dining rooms' along the bark. The nuthatch fixes more nuts than it normally requires and leaves behind a large number on tree trunks within its territory.

It might come back for them in winter. Then, the search for food takes up a great part of its day; tirelessly the nuthatch explores the crevices and trunks of its various food stores.

In winter the nuthatch will visit a feeding table where you have placed almonds, hazelnuts and walnuts all mixed in unsalted margarine or lard. It can compete for the food quite successfully with the tits however aggressive these may be.

Held as in a vice, a nut is opened by the nuthatch.

Nuts in fat attract nuthatches and tits.

36

A woodland bird, the nuthatch can become a regular visitor to gardens: it will feed from bird-tables and sometimes takes over nesting boxes.

A NESTING BOX

As it is a bird that likes to nest in enclosed dark places, it will readily make its home in a nesting box hanging in a tree. Place the box more than three metres from the ground. Use string rather than nails to fix it up so as not to damage the tree and, equally important, make sure it is out of reach of other animals, especially cats.

The nuthatch seals up all the slits of the nesting box with a mixture of mud and dung and, if the entrance is too big, it makes it smaller by plastering mud round it. Even if the nesting box is perfect, instinct drives the nuthatch to deposit pellets of mud inside it.

COMPETING FOR A NEST

A pair of nuthatches decided to take over the nest of some black woodpeckers, which are the size of small crows. The woodpeckers were pecking out pieces of wood from the nest gradually making it bigger, then went off to feed. While they were away, the nuthatches plastered up the entrance, which was much too big for them. With a powerful scream, the woodpeckers arrived and chased the nuthatches away. The woodpeckers then pulled away the fresh plaster, but not without some difficulty. As soon as the woodpeckers went away again, the nuthatches came back to start their work again.

After their work was demolished three times by the black woodpeckers and confronted with such giant birds, which were much too strong for them, the nuthatches finally gave up the battle and looked for another place in which to nest.

Ants

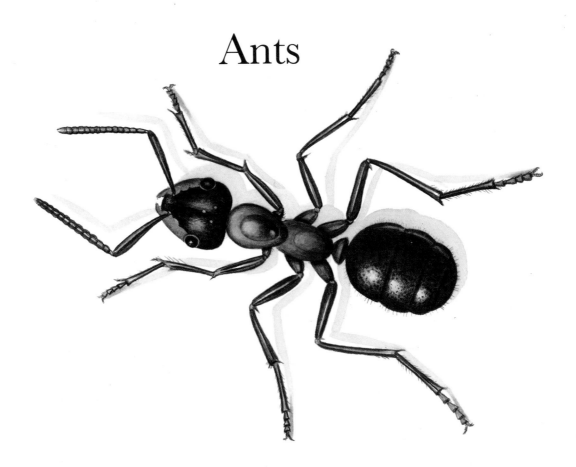

AN ORGANIZED SOCIETY

All ants live in a nest called an anthill, which comprises a large number of chambers and galleries.

In woods and forests you often come across the nest of the wood ant: a large swept-up heap of pine needles, twigs and refuse about a metre high. Other species have more discreet nests: dead wood, a mound of earth covered with grass, a hollow under a stone or brick.

Between 10 000 and 500 000 individuals live in a wood ants' nest. This population is made up of three different types of ant.

First, the workers. These are female ants that are wingless and sterile, that is to say females that cannot have young. Their life-span is between two and three months for those born during summer and a little longer for those born in autumn. It is the workers that build, tend and defend the nest. They are easily the most numerous within a population.

The second type of ant are the flying ants. These are born during the summer and comprise males and females that can breed. There are a few hundred of these in the nest.

Third is the queen ant, which lays eggs at regular intervals and can be double the size of each of the other ants.

AN ANT FARM

To find out about the underground activities of ants, you can build an ant farm. This demands great care as the slightest slit left open will allow the inhabitants to escape.

In spring, look out for anthills in the garden or the forest. After observing and making a note of the ants comings and goings, the paths they use and the food they carry, gather a few of them in the following manner:

With a spade or shovel, take some earth with its lodgers from different levels of the anthill. You must collect some workers, some pupae (often wrongly called eggs), and a queen, which you will usually find deep within the anthill.

Collect ants from only one colony and choose either black or wood ants; red ants cannot be bred in captivity. Empty the earth, insects and some twigs into the ant farm, where you have already put some loose earth, honey, sugar crystals, bread crumbs, water and a little container in which you have placed a cutting from a rose bush covered in aphids.

A FOOD WORKER

'Explorer' worker ants go out in search of food. They surround the food with scented droplets and go back to the nest leaving a trail of the same scent on the way. They 'tell' other worker ants of their find; ants communicate with one another by rubbing each other's antennae. A few minutes later a large number of ants arrive at the food and a two-way traffic starts between the nest and the food.

The explorers do not take part in the gathering of food. This is done by other workers. At the nest, the food is eaten by the adult insects or distributed to the larvae.

Ants will climb on branches covered in aphids. By rubbing the aphids with their antennae, the ants make these insects give out drops of sweet liquid, the honeydew. This the ants suck up

An ant farm

Collecting ants

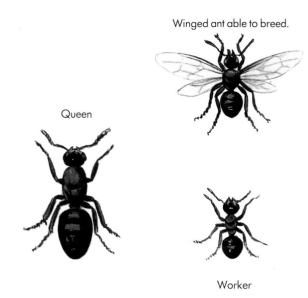

Winged ant able to breed.

Queen

Worker

The workers look after the pupae.

The dimensions of an ant farm can vary; the important thing is to preserve the principle of the two parts.

1 – Ventilation hole covered with wire mesh or a piece of net used for curtains.
2 – Communication holes between the anthill and the food.
3 – Drinking trough
4 – Hole to put in the food.

The earth of the nest must be moistened at regular intervals.

immediately. The ants are said to 'milk' the aphids, as this process is similar to the way we squeeze a cow's udders to obtain its milk.

A NEW COLONY

One stormy summer day the flying ants, males and females, take to the wing to mate. After mating, the males die almost immediately whereas the females – the queens – bite off their wings and each builds a nest, the start of a new colony.

After the birth of the first workers, the queen's only activity will be to lay more eggs. This she does at a rate of one egg every two minutes. The workers hatched from the first eggs come out of the nest, collect food and feed their mother. Before they hatched, the queen will have survived by eating some of her own eggs.

After a few days in the ant farm, the captive ants will have established various living levels and you will be able to see the 'royal chamber' and the queen inside it, the nursery with the larvae and the pupae, the cellars filled with food and sometimes a cemetery.

FORMIC ACID

If you move your hand over an anthill several times, you will cause pandemonium. The soldier-workers will emerge to defend the nest. Your hand will probably have acquired an unpleasant smell. This comes from the droplets of formic acid, a chemical emitted by the soldiers. When threatened, the ant curls its abdomen forward to squirt its enemy. An ant that does not belong to the colony will be immobilized and killed by the acid.

The Common Cuckoo

A SOLITARY WOODLAND DWELLER

About mid-April, without even seeing it you know it has arrived. The forest echoes with its "coo-coo" calls that are powerful enough to make you believe the bird is close by. As soon as it starts to court the female, its calls get more frantic, marking the bird's excitement.

Apart from the mating period, it is a solitary bird that you can sometimes catch a glimpse of as it flies across a clearing. It has a grey back and wings and distinctive grey and white barring on the underparts. It can often be mistaken for a sparrowhawk. Its legs look like those of a woodpecker, with two toes pointing forwards and two backwards.

The cuckoo eats insects, especially the larvae, but it will also eat worms and centipedes. Its favourite food is caterpillars. Cuckoos in southern Europe especially like processionary moth caterpillars. These make large silk communal webs that can be seen at the top of pine trees. The hairs of these caterpillars are particularly irritating but this does not worry the cuckoo. It swallows the caterpillars and collects the hairs on the lining of its stomach until the lining tissue looks like felt. It then spits out shreds of the tissue laden with hairs.

WHO TO GIVE ITS EGG TO?

The cuckoo is a parasite of other species of bird as it deposits its eggs in another's nest and leaves the upbringing of its young to the foster parents.

The hen cuckoo will watch the sparrows of an area to find where a pair of them have made their nest. The sparrows will react as if the cuckoo is a bird of prey; they will try to chase it away. The sparrows' aggressiveness is so great that they will even rush at and attack a stuffed cuckoo placed near their nest.

Taking advantage of the sparrows' first short absence, the female cuckoo lifts an egg out of their nest, swallows it or drops it, lays one of her own in its place and flies away all in a few seconds. Then it looks for other nests in which to lay eggs, one per nest. Each female specializes in taking advantage of one particular bird species; it seems to choose the same species by which it was reared.

By June the egg-laying is over and the singing has stopped. The cuckoo discreetly leaves in July, flying by night to its winter home in Africa.

ALWAYS THE FIRST

The young cuckoo's life is organized so that it succeeds in everything. It is the first bird to hatch out in the foster-nest as the cuckoo's egg needs a shorter incubation period than those of its host. Even if it hatches at the same time as the rest of the brood, the outcome is the same. An astonishing reflex action leads the young cuckoo, as soon as it is born, to evict the foster-parents' young from the nest. The baby cuckoo manoeuvres itself towards the bottom of the nest so that an egg or chick becomes balanced on its back, between the wings. It then hoists the egg or unfortunate creature over the edge of the nest, to be followed in turn by the others. Curiously the foster-parents look on with indifference.

Very small birds such as the robin or the reed warbler are able to feed a

The cuckoo hen makes room in a host's nest.

…and places its own egg inside.

The young cuckoo ejects the other eggs from the nest.

44

"Whoever has some money on hearing the cuckoo for the first time will be rich all year."

young cuckoo even though within a few weeks it will become ten times their size. It is a considerable task for them to fill the cuckoo's forever gaping orange throat with larvae and insects.

The young cuckoo soon gets too big for the nest, which starts to crumble under its weight. But even when after three weeks it starts to flit about on the ground or in the branches, its foster parents still keep feeding it, often having to perch on its back to be able to drop insects in the gaping beak. It lives off the foster parents until it feels confident enough to become independent and lead a cuckoo's solitary life.

To have its eggs incubated by other species the cuckoo goes to great lengths, but not always successfully. Some birds will not tolerate it: the blackcap heaves the cuckoo's egg over the side of its nest, the warbler abandons the invaded nest. It is estimated that out of fifteen or twenty eggs laid by the female cuckoo only one will hatch into a bird capable of undertaking the annual migration to Africa and back.

A TRADITIONAL BIRD

The cuckoo has inspired numerous popular traditions. Earthenware or wooden whistles with two holes are made that can reproduce its call. We play hide and seek calling out "coo-coo". In April, on hearing the cuckoo for the first time we feel the coins at the bottom of our pocket, hoping to be rich for the rest of the year.

Numerous objects have been named after the cuckoo: in Switzerland there is the cuckoo clock, in France a type of aircraft, in the British Isles plants such as the cuckoo flower, cuckoo pint and cuckoo's meat.

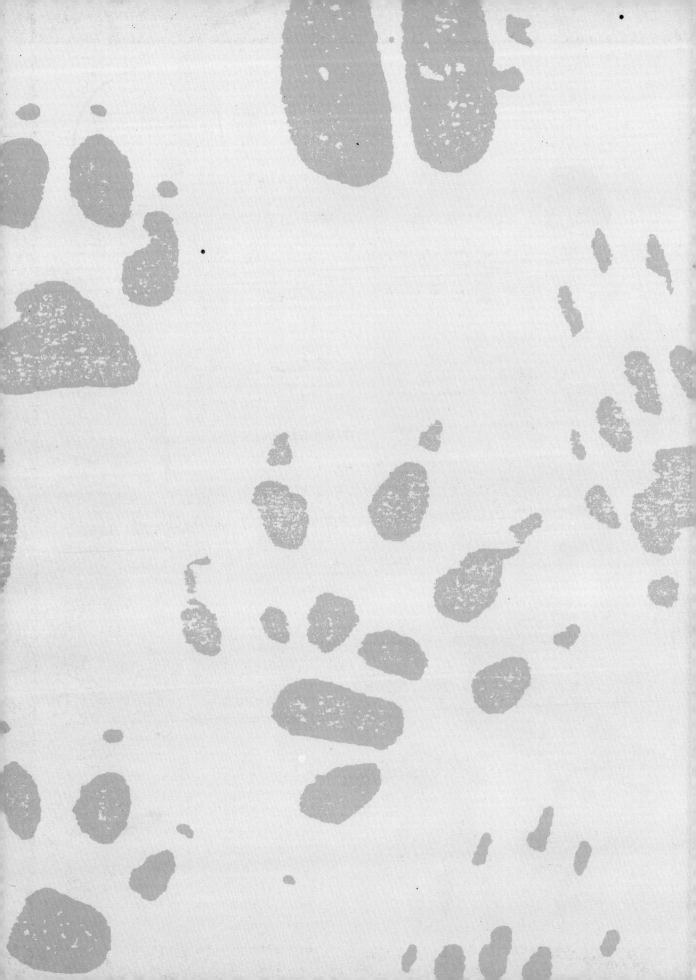

Other Teddy Bear Books by Exley:
Teddy Bear Quotations
Teddy Bears a Celebration
Teddy Lovers Address Book

Published simultaneously in 1995 by Exley Publications in Great Britain,
and Exley Giftbooks in the USA.

12 11 10 9 8 7 6 5 4 3 2

ISBN 1-85015-527-2

Edited by Helen Exley.
Illustrated by Juliette Clarke.
Typeset by Delta, Watford.
Printed and bound in Spain by Grafo, S.A. – Bilbao

Exley Publications Ltd, 16 Chalk Hill, Watford, Herts WD1 4BN, UK.
Exley Giftbooks, 232 Madison Avenue, Suite 1206, NY 10016, USA.

Acknowledgements: The publishers would like to thank the following for permission to
reproduce copyright material. They would be pleased to hear from any copyright
holders not here acknowledged. Gyles Brandreth: extract from "The Teddy Bear Craft
Book", published by Charles Letts & Co. Ltd. 1991; Peter Bull: extracts from "A Hug of
Teddy Bears", published by The Herbert Press/A & C Black; extract from "The Teddy
Bear Book", published by Hobby House Press Inc.; Gill Davies: extracts reproduced by
permission of the author © 1995 Gill Davies; Ted Menten: extracts from "The Teddy
Bear Lover's Companion" published by Courage Books, an imprint of Running Press ©
1991; Harald Nadolny and Yvonne Thalheim: extract from "Teddy Bears. A Complete
Step-By-Step Guide", published by Chancellor Press, a division of Reed Consumer
Books, 1993; Nanci van Roozendaal: extract from "Teddy Bears Past and Present"
published by Hobby House Press, 1991; Gustav Severin: extracts from "Teddy Bear"
published by Transedition Books/Andromeda Oxford Ltd. 1994. Reprinted by
permission Éditions Nathan, Paris.

—AN—
ILLUSTRATED
TEDDY BEAR
NOTEBOOK

JULIETTE CLARKE

EDITED BY

HELEN EXLEY

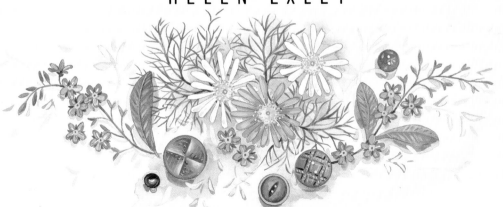

≡ EXLEY
NEW YORK • WATFORD, UK

... "Happy" seems to epitomize the sheer beauty and character we all seek in our teddy bears - gaze into those great big eyes and your heart just melts!

Margaret and Gerry Grey,
from "Teddy Bears"

*A teddy is a cuddle with
four paws on the end.*
Gill Davies

*Someone should invent a harness in which to hang bears
from the washing line. Pegs on the ears looks agonising.*
                                        Margot Burns

Wise teachers – well kind ones, anyway – invite teddies to school on the very first day.

James Fury

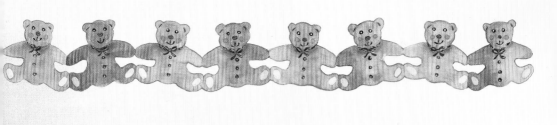

Am I alone in finding a row of Teddy Bears set up for sale at auction a sad sight? They are like lost pets.... They are toys that have lost their children, toys that recall childhood past and finished.
Mary Hillier

There are teddies that sit up ramrod straight
And those that cannot sit up at all
No matter how you prop them up
They slither, slide and fall
Ramrod teddies are fine, of course
And look tidy on a shelf
But because they need your help more
I like the floppy ones myself

Gill Davies

The world of the teddy bear is an innocent one, a world that "gives delight and hurts not", a world that appeals to all generations and all nationalities.

Gyles Brandreth,
from the foreword to "The Teddy Bear Craft Book"

They have all grown and gone...outwardly changed beyond belief. But Bear sits on the chest of drawers, just as he always has, and holds their childhood safe, until they need him once again.

Helen Thomson, b.1943

Did you know that the teddy has been called the world's most popular soft toy? That in Britain, 63 houses out of every 100 have one? That there are more than 140 million of them in the U.S.A.?

Leo Zanelli

*I think about the times during my travels that I've awakened
in the night in some strange hotel room, disoriented until I
recognize one of my bears sitting nearby, like a sentry. It
doesn't matter where I am; if there are teddies nearby, I know
that I am safe.*

*Ted Menten,
from "The Teddy Bear Lover's Companion"*

WITHOUT A BEAR. . . .

*A bedroom without a teddy
is like a face without a smile.*
                    Gill Davies

He [a teddy bear] is a constant link in a chain of love, his position and status similar to that of a pagan household god, protecting successive generations.

Geneviève and Gérard Picot,
from "Teddy Bears"

The secret, in my opinion, of the continued appeal of the Teddy is his immense ability to listen and understand.
  Peter Bull (1912-1984), from "Best of Teddy Bear and friends"

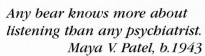

*Any bear knows more about
listening than any psychiatrist.
Maya V. Patel, b.1943*

Teddies have gone into battle on guns, tanks, and in haversacks. There is not a corner of the globe they have not penetrated. They have saved lives by intercepting bullets, breaking falls, and just being around. They've flown round the world, been drowned in floods, burned in concentration camps, and worshipped as totems.

Peter Bull (1912-1984),
from "The Teddy Bear Book"

Teddy Bears shouldn't sit in closets when there's a child around who will love them.　　　　*Janet Dailey, b.1944*

THROUGH THE HARD TIMES....

What a miracle life is, and how whimsical that in all their wonder and their pain, their confusion and their joy, human beings had the idea to create teddy bears to keep them company and help them make it through the hard times.

Ted Menten,
from "The Teddy Bear Lover's Companion"

Prescription for relief of tears and nervous tension: one teddy bear, taken as needed. No side effects, but the love may become addictive.

James D. Nelson

The good old teddy bear is still going strong. He'll still be with us in the next century because we cannot do without him. For some he's there to be collected, for others to be hugged and cuddled.

Gustav Severin (1925-1992),
from "Teddy Bear"

A Teddy bear can become the
object of any kind of love by any
kind of person. Out of a choice of
hundreds or even thousands of
teddies each person can find just
the right bear to love.

Helen Thomson, b.1943

At some point the day arrives when the child, now a grownup, starts rummaging around for the memories of their youth in general and for their old teddy in particular. The reunion awakens deeply slumbering emotions and the bear, this leftover from an untroubled childhood, is elevated to a place of honor. . . .

Gustav Severin (1925-1992),
from "Teddy Bear"

Every immaculate home needs a dilapidated bear sitting around somewhere – just to remind you that a home is for living in.

B.R. Meadows

Often [the relationship with a bear] can be almost closer than the one they have with their parents. For he (or she) can enter a secret world with Teddy. No demands, no regulations and, above all, a sympathetic and understanding friend to have constantly at one's elbow.

Peter Bull (1912-1984),
from "A Hug of Teddy Bears"

. . . bears are sought by young and old alike just to hug. They have to be soft, snuggly, and indestructible.

*Gustav Severin (1925-1992),
from "Teddy Bear"*

MINE

He may not be as beautiful
as lots of Teds you see
He isn't new with ribbons
or as big as big can be
He's small and old and tired
with a bandage round his knee
But he's really truly special
'Cos he all belongs to me

Gill Davies

All bears merit a Dignified Old Age.
                                    Peter Gray

*Bears have life breathed into them
by years of loving.*
    Marion C. Garretty, b.1917

A teddy is a friend
who is always waiting there
Soft and warm and smiling
a cuddly snuggly bear
Some people are like teddies
And one of them is you
You're snuggly, warm and comfy
but can I keep my teddy too?

Gill Davies

With their fur rubbed bald from loving hands, their ears resewn or replaced, their paw pads frayed and patched [teddy bears] make me feel like a child again, seeking love, understanding, and security from a hostile and frightening adult world.

Ted Menten,
from "The Teddy Bear Lover's Companion"

*Looking into the eyes of the Most-Loved Teddy Bear
contenders, I am smitten. But then I remember my
grandmother – a real teddy bear expert – and all she taught
me about love and how to choose a proper teddy bear.
I give each tousled bear the definitive test – a hug.
And the prize goes to that very special teddy bear that makes
me feel most loved.*

*Ted Menten,
from "The Teddy Bear Lover's Companion"*

A teddy bear appears to children as a kind of guardian angel in a shaggy coat and they won't do without its cuddly presence even when they are asleep. Nor does it bother them when their bear loses its hair and becomes unpresentable; quite the opposite: worn-off fur, patches, and other signs of age only serve to increase its charm and strengthen the inner bonds.

Gustav Severin (1925-1992),
from "Teddy Bear"

Some parents make the hideous error of getting rid of an old, battered and possibly smelly but beloved bear and substituting a brand new extremely expensive one. A child of four could tell them this is nothing short of criminal.

Peter Bull (1912-1984),
from "A Hug of Bears"

A bear does not go in for brains and hearts and bones and such. He hasn't room for them. He is packed tight with love.
                                    Pam Brown, b.1928

There is something remarkable about teddy bears. It has been my experience that I might have found myself grumpy – but then I simply chance to look at a bear and something happens. My mood changes, the furrowed brow disappears, I lift my head, and lo and behold it has happened! I find myself happy! I also see this happen over and over as other people respond to all kinds of bears, tiny, big, skinny, fat, silly, serious, primitive, sophisticated, you name it! People get happy!

Nanci van Roozendaal,
from "Teddy Bears Past and Present"

*You <u>know</u> his eyes are coloured glass.
Then why does he look so desperately
disconsolate when you go out and
leave him behind?*

Pam Brown, b.1928

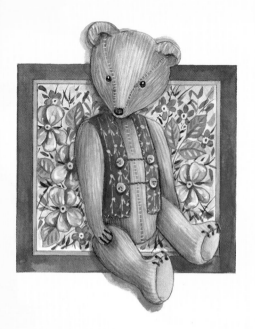

*Bears doze a little, but never
really sleep. They take their job
as Protectors very seriously.*
Mercia Tweedale, b.1915

...the teddy bear was born out of an act of kindness, nurtured by an artist's gentle wit, and fashioned by a physically handicapped toymaker to please her beloved nephew. Right from the start, the teddy bear represented the brightest side of human nature. Is it any wonder that over the decades, millions of us have embraced the kindly teddy bear, making him our constant companion and best friend?

Ted Menten,
from "The Teddy Bear Lover's Companion"

An advantage of a Teddy as a friend is that he will shoulder the blame for some misdemeanour committed by his owner. "It wasn't me," you will hear the child shout, "it was Teddy. Naughty, naughty Teddy!" And often as not this blatant lie will be accompanied by a sharpish blow or a throw across the room. Later, with luck, you will see the child apologizing to his friend and asking for forgiveness, which is readily given.

Peter Bull (1912-1984),
from "A Hug of Teddy Bears"

Long before I grew up, my teddy-bear taught me what love really meant – being there when you're needed.

Jim Nelson